Map of Gulf of Mexico showing states TX, LA, MS, AL, GA, FL and numbered viewing areas.

1. Santa Ana National Wildlife Refuge
2. Laguna Atascosa National Wildlife Refuge
3. Padre Island National Seashore
4. Aransas National Wildlife Refuge
5. Brazoria National Wildlife Refuge
6. High Island
7. Sabine National Wildlife Refuge
8. Lacassine National Wildlife Refuge
9. Grand Isla State Park
10. Delta National Wildlife Refuge
11. Gulf Islands National Seashore
12. Dauphin Island
13. Bon Secour National Wildlife Refuge
14. St. Andrews State Park
15. St. Vincent National Wildlife Refuge
16. Saint Marks National Wildlife Refuge
17. Honeymoon Island State Park
18. Sanibel Island
19. Everglades National Park
20. Florida Keys
21. Dry Tortugas National Park

GULF COAST BIRDS – A Waterproof Folding Guide to Familiar Species

Kavanagh/Leung

GULF COAST
BIRDS

A Waterproof Folding Guide to Familiar Species

WATERBIRDS

Common Loon
Gavia immer To 3 ft. (90 cm)
Winter / Summer

Eared Grebe
Podiceps nigricollis To 14 in. (35 cm)
Note black neck and golden ear tufts.

Pied-billed Grebe
Podilymbus podiceps
To 13 in. (33 cm)
Note banded white bill.

Canada Goose
Branta canadensis
To 43 in. (1.1 m)

Snow Goose
Chen caerulescens
To 31 in. (78 cm)

Redhead
Aythya americana
To 22 in. (55 cm)

Northern Pintail
Anas acuta
To 30 in. (75 cm)

Gadwall
Mareca strepera
To 23 in. (58 cm)

Ring-necked Duck
Aythya collaris To 18 in. (45 cm)
Note white ring near bill tip.

Lesser Scaup
Aythya affinis
To 18 in. (45 cm)

American Coot
Fulica americana To 16 in. (40 cm)

American Wigeon
Mareca americana
To 23 in. (58 cm)

WATERBIRDS

Mallard
Anas platyrhynchos
To 28 in. (70 cm)

Northern Shoveler
Spatula clypeata To 20 in. (50 cm)
Named for its large spatulate bill.

Blue-winged Teal
Spatula discors To 16 in. (40 cm)

Ruddy Duck
Oxyura jamaicensis
To 16 in. (40 cm)

Canvasback
Aythya valisineria To 2 ft. (60 cm)
Note sloping forehead and black bill.

Green-winged Teal
Anas crecca To 16 in. (40 cm)

Black-bellied Whistling-Duck
Dendrocygna autumnalis
To 21 in. (53 cm)

Fulvous Whistling-Duck
Dendrocygna bicolor To 20 in. (50 cm)
Tawny duck has a white side stripe.

Bufflehead
Bucephala albeola
To 15 in. (38 cm)

Common Goldeneye
Bucephala clangula
To 20 in. (50 cm)

Wood Duck
Aix sponsa
To 20 in. (50 cm)

WATERBIRDS

Red-breasted Merganser
Mergus serrator To 27 in. (68 cm)

Hooded Merganser
Lophodytes cucullatus
To 20 in. (50 cm)

Muscovy Duck
Cairina moschata To 32 in. (80 cm)
May be black or white. Males have 'warty' faces.

NEARSHORE BIRDS

American Woodcock
Scolopax minor
To 12 in. (30 cm)
Chunky, long-billed bird.

Common Gallinule
Gallinula galeata
To 14 in. (35 cm)

Purple Gallinule
Porphyrio martinicus
To 13 in. (33 cm)

Belted Kingfisher
Megaceryle alcyon
To 14 in. (35 cm)

Dunlin
Calidris alpina
To 9 in. (23 cm)
Note black belly patch.

Long-billed Dowitcher
Limnodromus scolopaceus
To 12 in. (30 cm)

Short-billed Dowitcher
Limnodromus griseus
To 12 in. (30 cm)
Feeds in a 'sewing machine' fashion while probing for food.

Whimbrel
Numenius phaeopus
To 20 in. (50 cm)
Note long decurved bill and striped crown.

Long-billed Curlew
Numenius americanus
To 26 in. (65 cm)
Long bill is slightly downturned.

NEARSHORE BIRDS

Willet
Tringa semipalmata
To 17 in. (43 cm)

Ruddy Turnstone
Arenaria interpres
To 10 in. (25 cm)

American Oystercatcher
Haematopus palliatus
To 20 in. (50 cm)

Greater Yellowlegs
Tringa melanoleuca
To 15 in. (38 cm)
Call is a 3-5 note whistle.

Lesser Yellowlegs
Tringa flavipes
To 10 in. (25 cm)
Call is a 1-3 note whistle.

Sanderling
Calidris alba
To 8 in. (20 cm)
Runs in and out with waves along shorelines.
Winter

Spotted Sandpiper
Actitis macularius
To 8 in. (20 cm)

Black-bellied Plover
Pluvialis squatarola
To 14 in. (35 cm)

Red Knot
Calidris canutus
To 12 in. (30 cm)
Plump, red-breasted shorebird.

Killdeer
Charadrius vociferus
To 12 in. (30 cm)
Note two breast bands.

Least Sandpiper
Calidris minutilla
To 6 in. (15 cm)

Wilson's Snipe
Gallinago delicata
To 12 in. (30 cm)

Semipalmated Plover
Charadrius semipalmatus
To 8 in. (20 cm)
Note single breast band.

Caspian Tern
Hydroprogne caspia
To 2 ft. (60 cm)
Bill is blood red.

Royal Tern
Thalasseus maximus
To 22 in. (55 cm)
Orange bill and black head crest are key field marks.

Winter

Forster's Tern
Sterna forsteri
To 15 in. (38 cm)
Note forked tail and white wing tips.

Ring-billed Gull
Larus delawarensis
To 20 in. (50 cm)
Bill has dark ring.

Bonaparte's Gull
Chroicocephalus philadelphia
To 14 in. (35 cm)
Small, black-headed gull.

Laughing Gull
Leucophaeus atricilla
To 18 in. (45 cm)
Note black head. Very common coastal species.

Common Tern
Sterna hirundo
To 15 in. (38 cm)
Note black cap and forked tail. Orange bill is black-tipped.

Herring Gull
Larus argentatus
To 26 in. (65 cm)
Legs are pinkish.

Black Skimmer
Rynchops niger
To 20 in. (50 cm)
Feeds by skimming over water with its lower bill cutting the water's surface to spear fish.

Brown Pelican
Pelecanus occidentalis
To 50 in. (1.3 m)

American Bittern
Botaurus lentiginosus
To 23 in. (58 cm)
Fairly common but secretive marsh bird has a distinctive call that sounds like a rusty water pump – oonk–KA-lunk.

American White Pelican
Pelecanus erythrorhynchos
To 5 ft. (1.5 m)

Yellow-crowned Night-Heron
Nyctanassa violacea
To 28 in. (70 cm)

Black-crowned Night-Heron
Nycticorax nycticorax
To 28 in. (70 cm)

Green Heron
Butorides virescens
To 22 in. (55 cm)

Great Blue Heron
Ardea herodias
To 4.5 ft. (1.4 m)
A white morph is distinguished from the similar great egret by its yellow bill and pale, yellow-gray legs.

White morph

American Avocet
Recurvirostra americana
To 20 in. (50 cm)

Little Blue Heron
Egretta caerulea
To 2 ft. (60 cm)

Tricolored Heron
Egretta tricolor
To 26 in. (65 cm)
Note white belly.

Reddish Egret
Egretta rufescens
To 30 in. (75 cm)

Great Egret
Ardea alba
To 38 in. (95 cm)
Note yellow bill and black feet.

Snowy Egret
Egretta thula
To 26 in. (65 cm)
Note black bill and yellow feet.

Cattle Egret
Bubulcus ibis
To 20 in. (50 cm)

Roseate Spoonbill
Platalea ajaja
To 32 in. (80 cm)
Bill is flattened at the tip.

Whooping Crane
Grus americana
To 4 ft. (1.2 m)
Endangered species winters in southern Texas.

Sandhill Crane
Antigone canadensis
To 4 ft. (1.2 m)

Black-necked Stilt
Himantopus mexicanus
To 17 in. (43 cm)

White Ibis
Eudocimus albus
To 28 in. (70 cm)

Juvenile

Double-crested Cormorant
Phalacrocorax auritus
To 3 ft. (90 cm)
Note orange-yellow throat patch.

Glossy Ibis
Plegadis falcinellus
To 26 in. (65 cm)
Note maroon neck.

Wood Stork
Mycteria americana
To 4 ft. (1.2 m)
Dark head is naked.

Magnificent Frigatebird
Fregata magnificens
To 40 in. (1 m)
Note red throat, long wingspan and forked tail. Females have a white throat.

Anhinga
Anhinga anhinga
To 3 ft. (90 cm)
Note long snake-like neck.

♂

Turkey Vulture
Cathartes aura
To 32 in. (80 cm)
Note red head and two-toned underwings.

Swallow-tailed Kite
Elanoides forficatus
To 2 ft. (60 cm)

Black Vulture
Coragyps atratus
To 27 in. (68 cm)

Red-tailed Hawk
Buteo jamaicensis
To 25 in. (63 cm)

Cooper's Hawk
Accipiter cooperii
To 20 in. (50 cm)
Note long, rounded white-tipped tail.

Red-shouldered Hawk
Buteo lineatus
To 22 in. (55 cm)
Note red shoulders and dark, banded tail.

American Kestrel
Falco sparverius
To 12 in. (30 cm)
Note small size and blue wings.

Osprey
Pandion haliaetus
To 2 ft. (60 cm)

Bald Eagle
Haliaeetus leucocephalus
To 40 in. (1 m)

Crested Caracara
Caracara cheriway
To 25 in. (63 cm)
Note red face and black head crest.

Great Horned Owl
Bubo virginianus
To 25 in. (63 cm)
Call is a loud – who-cooks-for-you? who-cooks-for-you-all?

Barred Owl
Strix varia
To 2 ft. (60 cm)
Call is resonant – hoo-HOO-hoooo.

Bronzed Cowbird
Molothrus aeneus
To 9 in. (23 cm)
Note red eyes.

Red-winged Blackbird
Agelaius phoeniceus
To 9 in. (23 cm)

American Crow
Corvus brachyrhynchos
To 22 in. (55 cm)

Boat-tailed Grackle
Quiscalus major
To 16 in. (40 cm)
Long tail is keel-shaped.

♀

Northern Mockingbird
Mimus polyglottos
To 11 in. (28 cm)

Common Grackle
Quiscalus quiscula
To 14 in. (35 cm)

European Starling
Sturnus vulgaris
To 8 in. (20 cm)

Ruby-throated Hummingbird
Archilochus colubris
To 3.5 in. (9 cm)

Brewer's Blackbird
Euphagus cyanocephalus
To 9 in. (23 cm)
Note yellow eyes.

White-winged Dove
Zenaida asiatica
To 12 in. (30 cm)
Note prominent white wing patches.

Brown-headed Cowbird
Molothrus ater
To 7 in. (18 cm)

Rock Pigeon
Columba livia
To 13 in. (33 cm)

Mourning Dove
Zenaida macroura
To 13 in. (33 cm)
Call is a mournful – ooah-woo-woo-woo.

Eurasian Collared-Dove
Streptopelia decaocto
To 11 in. (28 cm)

Brown Thrasher
Toxostoma rufum
To 12 in. (30 cm)

American Robin
Turdus migratorius
To 11 in. (28 cm)

Blue-grey Gnatcatcher
Polioptila caerulea
To 4.5 in. (11 cm)

Blue Jay
Cyanocitta cristata
To 14 in. (35 cm)

Eastern Bluebird
Sialia sialis
To 7 in. (18 cm)

Common Yellowthroat
Geothlypis trichas
To 5 in. (13 cm)

Loggerhead Shrike
Lanius ludovicianus
To 9 in. (23 cm)

White-eyed Vireo
Vireo griseus
To 5 in. (13 cm)
Note white eye and yellow 'spectacles.'

Seaside Sparrow
Ammodramus maritimus
To 6 in. (15 cm)

House Sparrow
Passer domesticus
To 6 in. (15 cm)

Dark-eyed Junco
Junco hyemalis
To 7 in. (18 cm)

White-throated Sparrow
Zonotrichia albicollis
To 7 in. (18 cm)

Eastern Towhee
Pipilo erythrophthalmus
To 9 in. (23 cm)

Northern Cardinal
Cardinalis cardinalis
To 9 in. (23 cm)

♂